SPONSORSHIP PAGE

THIS BOOK IS SPONSORED BY

....

....

AS A GIFT TO

....

....

ON THIS DAY

....

'Each one must give as he has decided in his heart,
not reluctantly or under compulsion,
for God loves a cheerful giver.'
(2 Corinthians 9:7, ESV)

BY PRAYER M. MADUEKE

PRAYERS TO MARRY WITHOUT DELAY

BOOK 1 OF 40 PRAYER GIANTS

PRAYER
PUBLICATIONS
UNITED STATES

FREE EBOOKS

In order to say a 'Thank You' for purchasing *Prayers To Marry Without Delay*, I offer these books to you in appreciation.

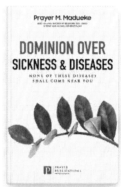
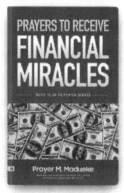

> **Click here or go to madueke.com/free-gift to download the eBooks now** <

MESSAGE FROM THE AUTHOR

PRAYER M. MADUEKE
CHRISTIAN AUTHOR

My name is Prayer Madueke, a spiritual warrior in the Lord's vineyard, an accomplished author, speaker, and expert on spiritual warfare and deliverance. I have published well over 100 books on every area of successful Christian living. I am an acclaimed family and relationship counselor with several titles dealing with critical areas in the lives of the children of God. I travel to several countries each year speaking and conducting deliverance sessions, breaking the yokes of demonic oppression and setting captives free.

It would be a delight to collaborate with you or your ministry in organized crusades, ceremonies, marriages and marriage seminars, special events, church ministration and fellowship for the advancement of God's kingdom here on earth.

You can find all my books on my website: madueke.com.

They have produced many testimonies and I want your testimony to be one too. God bless you.

CHRISTIAN COUNSELLING

We were created for a greater purpose than only survival and God wants us to live a full life.

If you need prayer or counselling, or if you have any other inquiries, please visit the counselling page on my website madueke.com/counselling to know when I will be available for a phone call.

EMAIL NEWSLETTER & ANNOUNCEMENTS

Never miss a message from me again! People who read my newsletters say that they have been one of the most important tools in their Christian walk. The best part is that a subscription is, and always will be, completely free. As a subscriber on my mailing list, you'll be the first to hear about my new book releases, be invited to my weekly prayer sessions, and get reminders about my blog posts and other helpful information.

To subscribe, please visit the newsletter page on my website madueke.com/newsletter.

DEDICATION

This book is dedicated to people who are trusting God to find their rightful spouse to build a Christian family. The Lord who sees your sincere dedication will answer your prayers Amen.

TABLE OF CONTENTS

Dedication .... *iv*

Chapter One

Seeking For A Right Partner 1

Chapter Two

The Purpose Of Marriage 5

Chapter Three

Power That Hinders Marriages 18

Chapter Four

Idolatry And Forsaking God 25

Warfare Section

Prayers To Marry Without Delay 31

ONE

SEEKING FOR A RIGHT PARTNER

Marriage is a legally recognized relationship, established by a civil or religious ceremony, between two people who intend to live together as sexual and domestic partners. In a marriage institution, a man and woman are legally joined together to start a new family.

The best place to start when planning to get married is to understand that marriage is for matured adults. That is why you must be matured physically, emotionally, socially and spiritually before you think of getting married. Likewise, marriage of convenience is not always the best type of marriage. It would be wrong to enter into any marriage relationship because of economic advantages, while disregarding the role of mutual affection and conviction. Marriages contracted on conveniences or solely for pragmatic reasons do not fulfill the spiritual purpose of marriage. Even an ant prepares itself for summer.

> Go to the ant, thou sluggard; consider her ways, and be wise: Which having no guide, overseer, or ruler, Provideth her meat in the summer, and gathereth her food in the harvest
>
> — PROVERBS 6:6-8

The choice of who to marry is never a decision to be done in haste. A lazy person that is looking for someone to marry because he or she wants to live comfortably would likely not fulfill God's purpose for marriage.

> Love not sleep, lest thou come to poverty; open thine eyes, and thou shalt be satisfied with bread
>
> — PROVERBS 20:13

Entering into marriage without needful knowledge and due preparation can be destructive. It is possible to accomplish an immediate need of comfort and satisfaction, but the problem is that you would have entered into a life of misery. Be mindful also, that marriage can provide momentary solutions to present problems, change of environment and temporal joy but also presents new set of challenges you have never imagined. Nevertheless, when you have the proper knowledge you needed, the new challenges will not overwhelm you.

Many people experience unfounded pleasures at the wake of their marriages instead of genuine intimacy and inner strength that sustain marriage. A temporal pleasure may not be very useful, especially when it is void of true and genuine love. Marriage should not be done in a rush. You need to develop some level of physical, temperamental, emotional, social and spiritual maturity in advance. Cultivate life of discipline, temperance, self-denial and selflessness, as these may be highly treasured by your spouse.

> [8]And the LORD God planted a garden eastward in Eden; and there he put the man whom he had formed. [15]And the LORD God took the man, and put him into the Garden of Eden to dress it and to keep it. [18]And the LORD God said, It is not good that the man should be alone; I will make him a help meet for him.

— GENESIS 2:8, 15, 18

Notice that Adam was in-charge of the garden before God made wife for him. He had a job already. He was the custodian of the garden. He knew God, and had intimate relationship with Him. God saw that it was not good for him to remain alone and made wife for him. Then, a big question arises - why do we need to marry?

TWO

THE PURPOSE OF MARRIAGE

God had a plan for establishing marriage union. That is why anyone who wants to marry must have idea of God's purpose in focus before deciding whom to marry. Unfortunately, many people have not bothered to find out God's purpose for marriage before entering into it.

> And the LORD God said, it is not good that the man should be alone; I will make him a help meet for him. And the rib, which the LORD God had taken from man, made he a woman, and brought her unto the man. Therefore shall a man leave his father and his mother, and shall cleave unto his wife: and they shall be one flesh.

— GENESIS 2:18, 22, 24

God concluded that it was not good that the man He made remained alone. In order to balance the equation, God created the woman. He used the rib, which He took from the man to make a woman. From the beginning, marriage has been part of God's plan, purpose and provision. God initiated this plan when man was at his original nature of purity.

> [27]So God created man in his own image, in the image of God created he him; male and female created he them. [28]And God blessed them, and God said unto them, Be fruitful, and multiply, and replenish the earth, and subdue it: and have dominion over the fish of the sea, and over the fowl of the air, and over every living thing that moveth upon the earth.
>
> — GENESIS 1:27, 28

Therefore, even at the height of our spirituality, we need to get married. God's blessings are complete upon a man when he is married, even though marriage is only necessary to earthly life, and has no part in eternal existence in heaven. Another important thing to observe is that God did not create many women for one man. He made one man and one woman. That is why men leave fathers and mothers and cleave to their wives to become one flesh.

> And he answered and said unto them, Have ye not read, that he which made them at the beginning made them male and female, And said, For this cause shall a man leave father and mother, and shall cleave to his wife: and they twain shall be one flesh? Wherefore they are no more twain, but one flesh. What therefore God hath joined together, let not man put asunder.
>
> — MATTHEW 19:4-6

> For the man is not of the woman; but the woman of the man. Neither was the man created for the woman; but the woman for the man. For this cause ought the woman to have power on her head because of the angels. Nevertheless neither is the man without the woman, neither the woman without the man, in the Lord. For as the woman is of the man, even

so is the man also by the woman; but all things
of God.

— 1 CORINTHIANS 11:8-12

God created the woman for the man and made them one. Therefore, the failure of the woman is the failure of the man, and the failure of the man is that of the woman. Lack of knowledge makes husband and wife to fight each other. Instead, husband and wife should succeed together. It is also foolishness for a woman to ruin the husband. God's plan is for both to make it together. Man needs a woman to succeed on earth because they were created as social beings to complement each other in marriage relationship.

God setteth the solitary in families: he bringeth
out those which are bound with chains: but the
rebellious dwell in a dry land.

— PSALMS 68:6

Lo, children are a heritage of the LORD: and the
fruit of the womb is his reward.

— PSALMS 127:3

God's ultimate purpose for instituting marriage is for a man and a woman to start a family, live as a family and succeed together as one family. Husband and wife are destined according to God's plan to bear children, rear and nurture them until they are matured enough to start their own families. Husband and wife are to put their faith together and fight barrenness.

> [5]And Moses commanded the children of Israel according to the word of the LORD, saying, The tribe of the sons of Joseph hath said well. [6]This is the thing which the LORD doth command concerning the daughters of Zelophehad, saying, Let them marry to whom they think best; only to the family of the tribe of their father shall they marry. [7]So shall not the inheritance of the children of Israel remove from tribe to tribe: for every one of the children of Israel shall keep himself to the inheritance of the tribe of his fathers. [8]And every daughter, that possesseth an inheritance in any tribe of the children of Israel, shall be wife unto one of the family of the tribe of her father, that the children of Israel may enjoy every man the inheritance of his fathers. [9]Neither shall the

inheritance remove from one tribe to another tribe; but every one of the tribes of the children of Israel shall keep himself to his own inheritance. [13]These are the commandments and the judgments, which the LORD commanded by the hand of Moses unto the children of Israel in the plains of Moab by Jordan near Jericho.

— NUMBERS 36:5-9, 13

Any power that attacks people's marriages is not from God. Individuals, families and the body of Christ must confront the scourge of late marriage or the powers that prevent matured adults from getting married. The presence of unmarried adults in the family is often very precarious. It has caused many problems especially in the developing world.

The spirit that causes adults not to be married must be confronted vigorously. All believers, including churches, must rise to fight this menace. Moses advised the tribes of the sons of Joseph to let the daughters of Zelophehad get married to whom they thought best. When one is due for marriage but is not married, there is an inclination that such person would be unhappy and this would affect people around him or her. In this way, such people become a burden to the family and community.

> And hath made of one blood all nations of men for to dwell on all the face of the earth, and hath determined the times before appointed, and the bounds of their habitation.
>
> — ACTS 17:26

Marriages must take place, in a right way and purpose, for people to live in peace in families, communities and nations. Marriage is fundamental to the stability and continuation of societies. When adults do not marry, there would be lack of peace in many families. In addition, when people refuse to leave and cleave, they eventually block the way for others to progress. However, unseen forces hold back many people's destinies. Even when such victims determine to marry, they cannot break loose from those forces holding them back. Others even go ahead to marry wrong people, who would later force them into unimaginable misery. Marriage is a necessity but requires wisdom and prayers.

> And the LORD God said, It is not good that the man should be alone; I will make him a help meet for him.
>
> — GENESIS 2:18

It is tragic to marry someone who cannot complement your destiny and work. People who find themselves in such cases often live in their families like strangers. A breakdown of marriage results in breakdown of families, communities and nations. This is the primary reason for never-ending divorce and separation cases, which bedevil nations of the world today. Ironically, many victims of divorce and separation would run back to their parents' homes to bother them. They fail to realize that after marriage, partners' top priority is each other and not parents.

> Two are better than one; because they have a good reward for their labor. For if they fall, the one will lift up his fellow: but woe to him that is alone when he falleth; for he hath not another to help him up. Again, if two lie together, then they have heat: but how can one be warm alone? And if one prevails against him, two shall

withstand him; and a threefold cord is not quickly broken. Better is a poor and a wise child than an old and foolish king, who will no more be admonished. For out of prison he cometh to reign; whereas also he that is born in his kingdom becometh poor.

— ECCLESIASTES 4:9-14

And did not he make one? Yet had he the residue of the spirit. And wherefore one? That he might seek a godly seed. Therefore take heed to your spirit, and let none deal treacherously against the wife of his youth.

— MALACHI 2:15

Regrettably, many people are convinced already that they were better off when they were not married than after marriage. Experiencing a few challenges in marriage forces weak men and women to conclude that marriage is a burden and evil. Probably, because of wrong choices here and there, they set their hearts on escaping from their marriages.

However, not allowing God to lead you to a right partner can result in regrets after getting married. The Scriptures equally made it clear that two is better than one because they have a good reward for their labor. Moreover, if one falls, the other will lift up his fellow. However, in many families today, there verse is the case. Because of irreconcilable differences, when both the man and his wife fall, none can lift up the other. This is also one of the reasons we have more widows on earth today. Couples defile the institution of marriage on daily basis. That is why one of the most effective witchcraft operations on earth today is the witchcraft of connecting two incompatible partners in marriage.

Let not a widow be taken into the number under threescore years old, having been the wife of one man, Well reported of for good works; if she have brought up children, if she have lodged strangers, if she have washed the saints' feet, if she have relieved the afflicted, if she have diligently followed every good work. But the younger widows refuse: for when they have begun to wax wanton against Christ, they will marry; Having damnation, because they have cast off their first faith. And withal they learn to be idle, wandering about from house to house; and not only idle, but tattlers also and busybodies, speaking things, which they ought

> not. I will therefore that the younger women
> marry, bear children, guide the house, give
> none occasion to the adversary to speak
> reproachfully.
>
> — 1 TIMOTHY 5:9-14

Many people have married more than twice and separated. Others were married, divorced and re-married. While some separated couples marry their right partners finally, others end up marrying their enemies. God's perfect will for marriage is one man, one wife. We have many matured single women who are not married. They move from one man to another, causing problems in families, communities and nations. Most of them are young, beautiful and more seductive than Delilah was.

They break homes, break hearts and cause a lot of hardship. When they break homes apart, the families enter into trouble and it affects the whole society. Many of these young ladies are idle, wandering from house to house, causing problems capable of tearing families and nations apart. They promote sexual sins and spread diseases on earth.

> Nevertheless, to avoid fornication, let every
> man have his own wife, and let every woman

have her own husband. Let the husband render unto the wife due benevolence: and likewise the wife unto the husband. The wife hath not power of her own body, but the husband: and likewise also the husband hath not power of his own body, but the wife. Defraud ye not one the other, except it be with consent for a time, that ye may give yourselves to fasting and prayer; and come together again, that Satan tempt you not for your incontinency.

— 1 CORINTHIANS 7:2-5

Some of these men and women possess strange fires of immorality from the marine realms of the spirit. Once you have sex with them, the love and sexual affections you have for your legally married partner transfers to them, and problems set in.

For this cause shall a man leave his father and mother, and shall be joined unto his wife, and they two shall be one flesh. This is a great mystery: but I speak concerning Christ and the church. Nevertheless let every one of you in particular so love his wife even as himself; and the wife see that she reverence her husband.

— EPHESIANS 5:31-33

THREE

POWER THAT HINDERS MARRIAGES

There are people that are marked before their birth to marry a demon-possessed personality. For such persons to get married to someone else other than the demon-possessed individual designated for them would be very difficult. They have to contend with wicked force of evil inheritance until they get their deliverance. However, you have to be born-again before you can prayerfully separate yourself from such evil captivity.

> The word of the LORD came also unto me,
> saying, Thou shalt not take thee a wife, neither
> shalt thou have sons or daughters in this place.

— JEREMIAH 16:1-2

Jeremiah sent the Word of God to a particular people to avoid marrying people from a particular place. He warned the people not to take wives from that community or have children with them. The all-seeing eyes of God had traced an evil mark upon the people from that particular place. This also means that one can be a true child of God, and yet lacks spiritual eyes to foresee evil. When a man or woman of God does not depend on God to make a choice for him or her in marriage, he or she is bound to make a costly mistake. However, this shall not be your portion, in the name of Jesus.

> O LORD, I know that the way of man is not in himself: it is not in man that walketh to direct his steps.
>
> — JEREMIAH 10:23

> And it came to pass, when they were come, that he looked on Eliab, and said, Surely the LORD'S anointed is before him. But the LORD said unto Samuel, Look not on his countenance, or on the

> height of his stature; because I have refused
> him: for the LORD seeth not as man seeth; for
> man looketh on the outward appearance, but
> the LORD looketh on the heart.
>
> — 1 SAMUEL 16:6-7

Man cannot direct his course on earth regardless of how righteous he is, and so needs to depend on God for direction. Many true children of God have made heart-breaking and painful mistakes in the area of marriage. While some thought that they have become matured adults and do not need God's direction, others believed the only problem they have is money. Once they get enough money to finance their marriage, they rush into a regrettable marriage. Jeremiah, with all his gifts, acknowledged that it is not in man's capacity to author his steps. If you do, you may actually marry someone that has evil inheritance and be doomed.

> For thus saith the LORD concerning the sons
> and concerning the daughters that are born in
> this place, and concerning their mothers that
> bare them, and concerning their fathers that
> begat them in this land; They shall die of

> grievous deaths; they shall not be lamented;
> neither shall they be buried; but they shall be as
> dung upon the face of the earth: and they shall
> be consumed by the sword, and by famine; and
> their carcasses shall be meat for the fowls of
> heaven, and for the beasts of the earth.
>
> — JEREMIAH 16:3-4

Accursed inheritance brings death verdicts upon some people even before they are born. It takes only God's grace and Word to erase such curses. If God directs you to marry in such place, He is also able to give you grace to deal with any inherited bondage. Let no man therefore do this unless under God's leadership. Today, many families are battling with diverse problems because they neglected God's leadership and went ahead to confront evil verdicts.

Many people go through unimaginable sufferings as a result. Such people suffer loss of things that makes one truly happy before finally losing their lives. They live in this world without any true helper. Though they are alive, they are not be better than dead people are. People avoid them as if they are dung on the face of the earth. Others reject and hate them without reasons. They suffer famine of every good thing that makes one happy. They are easy preys to witches and wizards and all manner of problems. These things sound like fairy tales but people go through them indeed.

Such people fail where others are succeeding. No matter how much faith you have, if God is not leading you, you must be careful when marrying, especially to people going through these unimaginable sufferings. For this reason also, any marriage of convenience would like backfire. However, the best assistance you can offer to such victims is to introduce them to Christ and probably teach them how to face spiritual battles of life regardless of how beautiful, handsome, rich or influential the person is. This is important because goodies, which are used to entice women, often disappear after marriage. Hence, the real battle of life starts immediately after marriage. This is not to scare you, but you must allow God be the stronghold of your marriage so you would not worry about challenges afterwards.

Appearance can be deceptive. Even Samuel, in all his gifts and relationship with God, made an error of judgment. He wanted to anoint Eliab because of his outward appearance. He preferred Eliab because of his excellent appearance, but God preferred David, a man after His heart. Do not allow beauty, certificates, money, wealth, good jobs and good things of life to hoodwink you in your choice of a partner. Depend on God and trust Him entirely.

¹⁶And I will bring the blind by a way that they knew not; I will lead them in paths that they have not known: I will make darkness light before them, and crooked things straight. These things will I do unto them, and not forsake them. ¹⁹Who is blind, but my servant? Or deaf, as my messenger that I sent? Who is blind as he that is perfect, and blind as the LORD'S servant? ²⁰Seeing many things, but thou observest not; opening the ears, but he heareth not.

— ISAIAH 42:16, 19-20

God regards us, His children, as blind even in all our righteousness. God promised in His Word to lead us in the paths that we have not known. He said that He would bring light in our darkness and make crooked things straight. Whatever decisions you take in marriage, make sure God is leading you. As a man, you can only see the beginning of a road but not the end. No matter how experienced you are, God is more experienced. No matter how old you are, God is older and wiser; He is the ancient of days, the beginning and the end. He is the Alpha and He is the Omega.

More so, you could have made so many mistakes in the past, but God cannot make any mistake. Trust God who knows how to lead you. Many people may appear good for marriage, but not all that appear excellent outwardly are worthy as your partner. Therefore, it would be heartbreaking and sad to marry someone who turns out to be incompatible.

Many people are in covenant with unseen powers. If you marry such people, you are doomed. In this book, I have provided suitable prayers to break you loose from marital bondage. You can also read one of my books titled *"Reality of Spirit Marriage."* That book will inform you about characteristics of men and women that you cannot afford to marry.

FOUR

IDOLATRY AND FORSAKING GOD

Idolatry means worshipping or walking after other gods, speaking in their names and setting them up in your heart. Other times, idolatry relates to covetousness, sensuality and sexuality. An idol is anything you put before God. Examples of idolatry include material possession, love of money, self or people above God.

> Mortify therefore your members which are
> upon the earth; fornication, uncleanness,
> inordinate affection, evil concupiscence, and
> covetousness, which is idolatry.
>
> — COLOSSIANS 3:5

And he said unto them, Take heed, and beware of covetousness: for a man's life consisteth not in the abundance of the things which he possesseth. And he spake a parable unto them, saying, The ground of a certain rich man brought forth plentifully: And he thought within himself, saying, What shall I do, because I have no room where to bestow my fruits? And he said, This will I do: I will pull down my barns, and build greater; and there will I bestow all my fruits and my goods. And I will say to my soul, Soul, thou hast much goods laid up for many years; take thine ease, eat, drink, and be merry. But God said unto him, Thou fool, this night thy soul shall be required of thee: then whose shall those things be, which thou hast provided? So is he that layeth up treasure for himself, and is not rich toward God.

— LUKE 12:15-21

God gave man a freedom of choice; you either choose to bow to God or to idols. Many spend their time, energy, and resources on gathering possessions at the expense of loving God and worshipping Him. While many people have not been married because of traces of idolatry in their foundation, others continue to practice it. Many others, who are married, are still going through unimaginable problems because of their link to evil worship.

> Of righteousness, because I go to my Father, and ye see me no more; Of judgment, because the prince of this world is judged. I have yet many things to say unto you, but ye cannot bear them now.
>
> — JOHN 16:10-12

Observing a tradition that contradicts God's Word in your marriage is an open invitation to demons to come into your marriage.

> Beware lest any man spoil you through philosophy and vain deceit, after the tradition of men, after the rudiments of the world, and not after Christ.
>
> — COLOSSIANS 2:8

God removes His protection upon your marriage when you engage in idolatry and forsake God. Satan has released many sexual demons to attack families. The only way to marry and remain happy is through total repentance and warfare. No one can marry and enjoy God's presence without breaking covenant with evil spirits and their agents, and then enter into covenant with God.

> And Samuel spake unto all the house of Israel, saying, If ye do return unto the LORD with all your hearts, then put away the strange gods and Ashtaroth from among you, and prepare your hearts unto the LORD, and serve him only: and he will deliver you out of the hand of the Philistines. Then the children of Israel did put away Baalim and Ashtaroth, and served the LORD only.
>
> — 1 SAMUEL 7:3-4

You must return to God in repentance; forsake your sins and cleave to God. You must prepare your heart and serve God only. You must hate sin in its entirety and love God, His Word and

His children. After this, you have to go into prayers of warfare to resist the devil.

> Submit yourselves therefore to God. Resist the devil, and he will flee from you.
>
> — JAMES 4:7

Prayers in this book will provide a good starting point for you to get to a level that will be too hot for your enemy to handle. By the grace and mercy of God, you will surely recover all your loss and marry to the glory of God.

1. The kind of prayers you are expected to pray -
1. Prayers against evil spirits that hinder marriages.
2. Prayers to cast out demons that resist your marriage.
3. Prayers to frustrate powers warring against your marriage.
4. Prayers to invoke the power of God to appear in the battlefield for your sake.
5. Prayers to destroy evil yoke of captivity and inheritance.
6. Prayers to command evil marks in your body to disappear.
7. Prayers to break inherited covenant and curses.
8. Prayers to command curses in your life to expire.
9. Prayers to ask for God's mercy upon you.

10. Prayers to silence evil voices crying against your marriage.

11. Prayers to command your spouse to appear by force.

12. Prayers to strengthen your faith in God and confess positively.

WARFARE SECTION

PRAYERS TO MARRY WITHOUT DELAY

And the LORD God said, It is not good that the man should be alone; I will make him a help meet for him

— GENESIS 2:18

Marriage is honorable in all, and the bed undefiled: but whoremongers and adulterers God will judge.

— HEBREWS 13:4

Begin with praise and worship

Any power that stands against my marriage, be frustrated, in the name of Jesus. Let maturity I needed to demonstrate before marriage manifest by force, in the name of Jesus. Let every property of devil in my life that is preventing my marriage catch fire, in the name of Jesus. Every satanic embargo that was placed upon my marriage, be lifted, in the name of Jesus. Father Lord, help me to get everything I needed to get before I marry, in the name of Jesus. Every weapon against my marriage, catch fire, in the name of Jesus. Any problem that is designed to make me miserable, I reject you, in the name of Jesus. I break and loose myself from any marriage devil is planning for me, in the name of Jesus. Any satanic offer that is enticing me to marry a wrong person, I reject you, in the name of Jesus. Father Lord, empower me to be fit in every area of my life before I marry, in the name of Jesus. Blood of Jesus, speak my right partner into existence, in the name of Jesus. Every enemy of God's will for my marriage, be disgraced, in the name of Jesus. O Lord, give me a better job that will sustain my marriage, in the name of Jesus. Let the perfect will of God for my marriage manifest, in the name of Jesus. Let everything aspect of my life embrace Jesus before my marriage, in the name of Jesus. O Lord, make my partner and I compatible, in the name of Jesus. O Lord, give me Your own perfect choice that will make my life complete, in the name of Jesus. Let my marriage usher the blessings of God into my life, in the name of Jesus. I refuse to marry my enemy, in the name of Jesus.

Pray in tongues and the language you understand.

THANK YOU!

I'd like to use this time to thank you for purchasing my books and helping my ministry and work. Any copy of my book you buy helps to fund my ministry and family, as well as offering much-needed inspiration to keep writing. My family and I are very thankful, and we take your assistance very seriously.

You have already accomplished so much, but I would appreciate an honest review of some of my books through the link below. This is critical since reviews reflect how much an author's work is respected.

Please visit https://www.amazon.com/review/create-review?asin=B09TDSFYCH or CLICK HERE TO LEAVE A REVIEW

Please be aware that I read and value all comments and reviews. You can always post a review even though you haven't finished the book yet, and then edit your reviews later.

Once again, here is the link:

Please visit https://www.amazon.com/review/create-review?asin=B09TDSFYCH or CLICK HERE TO LEAVE A REVIEW

Thank you so much as you spare a precious moment of your time and may God bless you and meet you at the very point of your need.

You can also send me an email to prayermadu@yahoo.com if you encounter any difficulty while writing your review.

OTHER BOOKS BY PRAYER MADUEKE

1. 100 Days Prayers to Wake Up Your Lazarus

2. 15 Deliverance Steps to Everlasting Life

3. 21/40 Nights of Decrees and Your Enemies Will Surrender

4. 35 Deliverance Steps to Everlasting Rest

5. 35 Special Dangerous Decrees

6. 40 Prayer Giants

7. Alone with God

8. Americans, May I Have Your Attention Please

9. Avoid Academic Defeats

10. Because You Are Living Abroad

11. Biafra of My Dream

12. Breaking Evil Yokes

13. Call to Renew Covenant

14. Command the Morning, Day and Night

15. Community Liberation and Solemn Assembly

16. Comprehensive Deliverance

17. Confront and Conquer Your Enemy

18. Contemporary Politicians' Prayers for Nation Building

19. Crossing the Hurdles

20. Dangerous Decrees to Destroy Your Destroyers (Series)

21. Dealing with Institutional Altars

22. Deliverance by Alpha and Omega

23.   Deliverance from Academic Defeats

24.   Deliverance from Compromise

25.   Deliverance from Luke warmness

26.   Deliverance from The Devil and His Agents

27.   Deliverance from The Spirit of Jezebel

28.   Deliverance Letters 1

29.   Deliverance Letters 2

30.   Deliverance Through Warning in Advance

31.   Evil Summon

32.   Foundation Exposed (Part 1)

33.   Foundations Exposed (Part 2)

34.   Healing Covenant

35.   International Women's Prayer Network

36.   Leviathan The Beast

37.   Ministers Empowerment Prayer Network

38.   More Kingdoms to Conquer

39.   Organized Student in a Disorganized School

40.   Pray for a New Nigeria

41.   Pray for Jamaica

42.   Pray for Trump, America, Israel and Yourself

43.   Pray for Your Country

44.   Pray for Your Pastor and Yourself

45.   Prayer Campaign for a Better Ghana

46.   Prayer Campaign for a Better Kenya

47.   Prayer Campaign for Nigeria

48.   Prayer Campaign for Uganda

49. Prayer Retreat

50. Prayers Against Premature Death

51. Prayers Against Satanic Oppression

52. Prayers for a Happy Married Life

53. Prayers for a Job Interview

54. Prayers for a Successful Career

55. Prayers for Academic Success

56. Prayers for an Excellent Job

57. Prayers for Breakthrough in Your Business

58. Prayers for Children and Youths

59. Prayers for Christmas

60. Prayers for College and University Students

61. Prayers for Conception and Power to Retain

62. Prayers for Deliverance

63. Prayers for Fertility in Your Marriage

64. Prayers for Financial Breakthrough

65. Prayers for Good Health

66. Prayers for Marriage and Family

67. Prayers for Marriages in Distress

68. Prayers for Mercy

69. Prayers for Nation Building

70. Prayers for Newly Married Couple

71. Prayers for Overcoming Attitude Problem

72. Prayers for Political Excellence and Veteran Politicians (Prayers for Nation Building Book 2)

73. Prayers for Pregnant Women

74. Prayers for Restoration of Peace in Marriage

75. Prayers for Sound Sleep and Rest

76. Prayers for Success in Examination

77. Prayers for Widows and Orphans

78. Prayers for Your Children's Deliverance

79. Prayers to Buy a Home and Settle Down

80. Prayers to Conceive and Bear Children

81. Prayers to Deliver Your Child Safely

82. Prayers to End a Prolonged Pregnancy

83. Prayers to Enjoy Your Wealth and Riches

84. Prayers to Experience Love in Your Marriage

85. Prayers to Get Married Happily

86. Prayers to Heal Broken Relationship

87. Prayers to Keep Your Marriage Out of Trouble

88. Prayers to Live an Excellent Life

89. Prayers to Live and End Your Life Well

90. Prayers to Marry Without Delay

91. Prayers to Overcome an Evil Habit

92. Prayers to Overcome Attitude Problems

93. Prayers to Overcome Miscarriage

94. Prayers to Pray During Honeymoon

95. Prayers to Preserve Your Marriage

96. Prayers to Prevent Separation of Couples

97. Prayers to Progress in Your Career

98. Prayers to Raise Godly Children

99. Prayers to Receive Financial Miracle

100. Prayers to Retain Your Pregnancy

101. Prayers to Triumph Over Divorce

102. Queen of Heaven: Wife of Satan

103. School for Children Teachers

104. School for Church Workers

105. School for Women of Purpose: Women

106. School for Youths and Students

107. School of Deliverance with Eternity in View

108. School of Ministry for Ministers in Ministry

109. School of Prayer

110. Speaking Things into Existence (Series)

111. Special Prayers in His Presence

112. Tears in Prison: Prisoners of Hope

113. The First Deliverance

114. The Operation of the Woman That Sit Upon Many Waters

115. The Philosophy of Deliverance

116. The Reality of Spirit Marriage

117. The Sword of New Testament Deliverance

118. Two Prosperities

119. Upon All These Prayers

120. Veteran Politicians' Prayers for Nation Building

121. Welcome to Campus

122. When Evil Altars Are Multiplied

123. When I Grow Up Visions

124. You Are a Man's Wife

125.   Your Dream Directory

126.   Youths, May I Have Your Attention Please?

FREE EBOOKS

In order to say a 'Thank You' for purchasing *Prayers To Marry Without Delay*, I offer these books to you in appreciation.

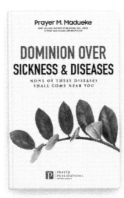
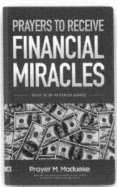

> **Click here or go to madueke.com/free-gift to download the eBooks now** <

CHRISTIAN COUNSELLING

We were created for a greater purpose than only survival and God wants us to live a full life.

If you need prayer or counselling, or if you have any other inquiries, please visit the counselling page on my website madueke.com/counselling to know when I will be available for a phone call.

EMAIL NEWSLETTER & ANNOUNCEMENTS

Never miss a message from me again! People who read my newsletters say that they have been one of the most important tools in their Christian walk. The best part is that a subscription is, and always will be, completely free. As a subscriber on my mailing list, you'll be the first to hear about my new book releases, be invited to my weekly prayer sessions, and get reminders about my blog posts and other helpful information.

To subscribe, please visit the newsletter page on my website madueke.com/newsletter.

AN INVITATION TO BECOME A MINISTRY PARTNER

In response to several calls from readers of my books on how to collaborate with this ministry, we are grateful to provide our ministry's bank details.

Be assured that our continued prayers for you will be answered according to God's Word, and as you remain faithful by sowing seeds of faith, God will never forget your labors of love in Christ Jesus.

Send your Seeds to:

In Nigeria & Africa

Bank Name: **Access Bank**

Account Name: **Prayer Emancipation Missions**

Account Number: **0692638220**

In the United States & the rest of the World

Bank Name: **Bank of America**

Account Name: **Roseline C. Madueke**

Account Number: **483079070578**

You can also visit the donation page on my website to donate online: www.madueke.com/donate.

Made in the USA
Middletown, DE
24 February 2023